A SINGLE GIRL'S GUIDE
TO FINDING MR. RIGHT

IS HE A

MAN

OR JUST ANOTHER

GUY?

GARY & MERRILEE LEWIS

DEDICATION

To Tiffany, Jennifer, and Mikayla

with love.

Acknowledgements

We give thanks to God for the relationships He has given us and the way He works in our lives. We say thank you to our mothers and fathers for their influence on our lives.

Thanks go to Jason Milliken, our publishing friend who shared our enthusiasm for the project. Also thanks to the other close friends who lent encouragement along the way.

Table of Contents

Foreword

This is a book about wisdom. Wisdom for living, and for life. It is a book for girls of all ages, for any woman who wants to live a life of abundance and happiness.

In writing this book, we went to the fountain of wisdom, the Holy Bible. Specifically, we went to Proverbs, a book written by the wisest man who ever lived—King Solomon.

After Solomon ascended to the throne of Israel, he asked the Lord for one thing above all else.

Now, O Lord my God, you have made your servant king in place of my father David. But I am only a little child and do not know how to carry out my duties. Your servant is here among the people you have chosen, a great people, too numerous to count or number. So give your servant a discerning heart to govern your people and to distinguish between right and wrong. For who is able to govern this great people of yours? (I Kings 3:7-9)

So God gave him wisdom, more than any man before or after. Because he did not ask for wealth or power or the death of his enemies, God blessed him with wealth and honor and gave him long life.

Because God, through Solomon, left His lessons for life in the Holy Bible, you can benefit from the same wisdom the Lord gave King Solomon.

Are you dating? Are you considering a possible marriage partner? Are you engaged or soon to be engaged? Are you married? Or divorced? There is something here for you.

This book will help you discern the difference between guys and men. It will teach you how to tell them apart. There are fundamental differences. Some guys are becoming men, maturing. Some guys will never grow up. The latter will steal your youth, your happiness, and your chance for security. It is important that you learn the difference.

The foolish let their feelings dictate plans for their future. Yes it's true. Being in love can make you stupid. And being in love with the wrong person can ruin your life.

Don't be a slave to your feelings. Apply wisdom and logic as you wait for a life mate. Use this book to help you gain a different perspective on love relationships.

This book does not constitute God's full counsel. Instead, it examines a portion of God's word as it relates to wisdom for living in relationships. Success in life is achieved through a personal relationship with God. Pray and read your Bible daily to find God's perfect will for your life.

Before you read any further, ask the Lord for a discerning heart; ask Him to help you make wise decisions. Wait on the Lord.

Chapter One

A New You

Have you desired to meet Mr. Right? Have you imagined what he would be like, this man that God has prepared for you?

To desire a relationship of loving and being loved in return is natural. It's how God made us.

Why is it important to discern God's will for your life? Why is it so important to make the right choice in a mate? It is important because the wrong choice can have serious consequences for the rest of your life.

You see, many guys never grow up. They never find the self-discipline or the external discipline (such as the military, personal accomplishments, or a demanding job) that turns them from boys to men. They become predators, parasites, or prey. You need to be prepared.

Predators are the guys who use women to satisfy their own appetites for money, sex, and power. They move from one woman to the next. Often, they are, in fact, women-haters—though they are seldom without a woman.

Parasites are the guys who never grew out of the need for a mother. They attach themselves to someone who will work for them so they don't have to work. Someone who will make their decisions for them so they don't have to think. Don't be that someone.

The prey are the guys who let life happen to them. They are often in trouble with the law or with credit card companies. They are vulnerable to the suggestions of others and easily manipulated.

There is something deceptively attractive about predators, parasites, and prey. They make women feel needed. It's true that these guys need a woman, but it is an unhealthy need and is based on their own inadequacies and selfish desires. Their need for a woman is not based on true love.

As His child, His creation, God desires to give you His best—a perfect complement to the person that you are or the person that He wants you to become.

From the time I was a child, I've watched my parents' relationship and the relationships of my uncles and aunts. Some of them made mistakes in timing and in choosing a mate. And some were perfectly matched.

I saw that marriage is for life. I began to recognize how important it is to make the right decision in a marriage partner. And to wait for the right timing.

I prayed that God would provide the mate that would be a complement to my personality. I prayed that He would give me the person with whom I could grow in the knowledge of Him.

When I first began to date, God showed me various personality types. He showed me possible life partners with whom I could live happily and those whose personalities did not fit mine.

I value those relationships, the experiences that God brought me through, and the lessons they taught me. They helped me to appreciate the partner that He finally gave me in His timing.

I learned that God was shaping me! He wanted me to be the right partner for my mate.

A good marriage is the wedding of two individuals who learn to live together in harmony, whether the goals of the individuals complement each other or not. Each partner grows in their respect for the other and their desire to please the other. Each learns to love their partner more as they grow old together.

God wants that type of relationship for you. But

He wants you to ask Him for it, to recognize Him as the ultimate authority in your life. God gives us what we need, but only when we ask for it.

Ask God for help in choosing a life partner. And ask Him to shape your life so that you can be the right life partner for the one God brings you.

Picture yourself living in marriage with the man God picked for you. Are you ready for him? Do you have the life skills needed to be the perfect mate? Can you balance a checkbook? Can you speak with knowledge about a number of subjects? Can you learn to enjoy activities you have never tried before?

How can you be the right match for your future mate? Practice seeing circumstances through the eyes of someone with an opposing viewpoint. How might you react if the roles were reversed?

Are you used to fine things? Your husband may not be as wealthy as your parents. Learn to "make do" with less and to be content. Learn to live within a budget. When you need to buy a big-ticket item, shop around and get a bargain.

If you don't know how to cook, learn the recipes for a few basic meals. Buy a good cookbook. Learn to enjoy cooking if you do not already.

Bringing these qualities to a marriage will not only endear Mr. Right to you, but will honor him once you have committed your lives to each other.

Go to God in prayer and ask Him to make you a new person. The woman He wants you to be.

> *Father,*
>
> *Thank you for caring for me. Thank you for wanting only the best for me. Oh Lord, I know I am a sinner. Forgive me. I know I am weak. Make me strong in You. Search my heart, Oh Lord, and show me the sin that I have not recognized that I might repent of it. Give me discernment. Make me the woman you want me to be.*
>
> *Amen*

CHAPTER TWO

A Blueprint for Your Future

*A*s *a ring of gold in a swine's snout, so is a beautiful woman who lacks discretion.* (Proverbs 11:22 NASB)

How many times have you seen a girl—pretty or plain, sharp and vivacious—walking hand in hand with a boy—ill-dressed, unshaven, grouchy? Don't you ask yourself what she sees in him?

Now take a look ten years into the future. What do you see? The same girl, her senses dulled by a decade of living with a guy who doesn't appreciate her. You see a guy—grown from a boy into a guy—who will never become a man because his woman never encouraged him to grow up and make something of himself before she gave him her love.

You see her children—ill-dressed, undisciplined, suffering from abuse or a lack of protection—the result of a marriage/shack-up relationship with the wrong guy. You see a woman, forced to be the bread-winner because her guy can't hold down a job.

Far-fetched? We don't think so. Look around when you walk down the street. You'll see the evidence everywhere. Don't let it happen to you.

As you read this book, remember that girl and the person she became. Set a higher ideal for yourself.

Think of this book as a blueprint for a new building. A building you have never been in before. Study the blueprint. Don't you want the suite on the top floor? You can't get there unless you climb the stairs.

On the ground floor, you find squalor. You find abusive relationships, drugs, alcoholism, and divorce.

You find unhappy single moms raising children without their fathers—girls who settled for less. You find an endless cycle of debt, self-doubt, and fear.

By walking up these stairs and away from the guys who want to keep you on the ground, you force those same guys to climb higher if they wish to follow. In short, *you* elevate *them*.

On the top floor, you will find quality of life. Up here, you help create your own happiness, your own way. You make your own decisions. Life reacts to you. You are living within God's plan. Mr. Right will be there. In fact, you may have to choose from several men, because real men recognize quality when they see it.

By wisdom a house is built, and through understanding it is established; through knowledge its rooms are filled with rare and beautiful treasures. (Proverbs 24:3-4)

Don't settle for the ground floor. Climb the stairs. Your life depends on it.

CHAPTER THREE

A Real Life Example

Amy was a pretty girl. Everybody said so. As she became a young lady, she began to attract the attention of the boys at church. She began dating. One night, she allowed herself to go too far.

A few weeks later, he broke up with her. She was hurt. When she saw him again, she had trouble looking him in the eye. He treated her as if she didn't exist.

She kept looking for that feeling again. The feeling of being wanted, of mattering to someone. She began to try too hard.

Amy watched her sister fall in love. She watched

their relationship blossom. When the time was right, her sister was married.

Amy was happy for her sister, but a part of her was jealous too. Amy lived at home with mom and dad. Instead of saving money, she bought clothes and a new car. When she lost her job, her credit cards supported her lifestyle—for awhile.

Then one day she met Spence. He drove a new sports car and made good money as an engineer. Her parents objected. He was divorced, didn't share her faith, and was deeply in debt. Soon, she was keeping her toothbrush at his house.

A few weeks later, she moved in. They would try each other out for awhile, like customers walking around the shoe store, trying on loafers. They grew comfortable; then they married.

Amy brought her baggage to the relationship. Her spending habits hadn't changed and her ideal of the perfect relationship was forming. But she could see that they weren't there yet. The guy wasn't serving enough. After all, he expected her to work outside the home also. Why did she need to do the laundry, cook, *and* do dishes? He must do the laundry and the dishes. She could cook.

Spence brought his own baggage to the marriage. By their first anniversary he was throwing up his hands. The woman was his—no need to keep the weight off anymore. Besides, he was so tired from working overtime, doing laundry and dishes that he didn't have the energy to workout anymore.

The trouble was that no one ever taught Amy how to tell the difference between a guy and a man. She wanted a wedding ring. And no one ever taught Spencer what being a man was all about. He wanted a warm bed and a woman who would make him feel like a man.

If there is one quality that sets a guy apart from a man it is self-indulgence. Guys want to please themselves. When that fails, they look for a woman who exists just to bring them pleasure.

Self-indulgence is most often found in the sons of dominant women. If a son is raised by a mother whose husband is a workaholic or has left the home, the boy may grow into a guy who seeks the comfort and security he had with mom—plus the added benefits of sex. What a combination! And there are plenty of needy girls out there who will provide this for them. Don't be one of them.

A self-indulgent husband will use you and control you. When he grows bored with the relationship, he will move on to another—regardless of his marital status. He will be vulnerable to overwork, pornography, alcohol, and drugs.

If you bring his children into the world, you will

be tied to him for life. If you have his children, they will likely behave as he did.

Amy's story isn't unique, it happens every day. But where did she go wrong? First, she picked someone who had failed in marriage already. Second, he didn't support her religious beliefs. Third, he had high consumer debt. Fourth, he encouraged her move in to his home without a wedding ring.

If you can see he isn't marriage material, don't even let him court you. Don't let what happened to Amy, happen to you. God wants His best for you.

CHAPTER FOUR

Why You Shouldn't Date Guys

D ating and courtship are not for fun. That's not to say that dating can't be fun—it can be. When you pick a man whose ideals match yours, who appreciates you for the woman that God made you to be, who sees the potential of a lasting, lifelong companion in you, it doesn't matter whether you are sharing a sundae in an ice cream parlor or cutting new powder on your snow skis. Just being with him is fun.

Spend time with the type of man with whom you can see yourself living for the rest of your life. When you date "just for fun" you are playing a dangerous game of Russian Roulette with your future.

Nobody explained this to Dakota. Or at least she didn't listen. She dated Kevin for six months, then became intimate with him. He was full of fire and jealous of her time. He made her feel wanted. But he was given to mood swings and even dangerous. When she finally realized that he was not the man with whom she should spend her life, she ended the relationship. She should have moved out of town.

He followed her everywhere she went. He drove by her house at all hours of the day and night. When she went on a date with someone else, he was in the background, watching.

One night she went to a party with some friends. Kevin was there. He took her outside because he wanted to talk, in private. They sat in his car. When he wanted to go for a drive, she said no. He locked the door before she could get out.

He took her out of town and up a gravel road, far away from the party and from anyone who might see what he intended. Ten miles from town, he stopped the car and pulled her out. No one heard her screams. No one was there to help. He beat her as she cried out for him to stop. Finally he relented.

Dakota staggered back to the car and climbed in while Kevin raged, pacing back and forth in the road. Suddenly, she noticed that he had left the keys in the ignition. She slammed the door and hit the automatic lock button. Sliding into the driver's seat, she started the car and headed back to town under the light of a quarter moon, leaving Kevin standing alone in the trees.

Back in town, she called the police who picked Kevin up at the edge of town—after his long walk. He spent the rest of the week in jail.

If you are dating someone who is angry or abusive— verbally or physically—your life is in danger. You deserve better. Leave him in your rearview mirror.

If you believe that marriage is in your future, believe that somewhere, there is a man that God is preparing for you. Be patient. Be the woman that God wants you to be and He will provide.

Don't automatically say "yes" to a date until you have asked yourself if this might be a man with whom you could trust your children, a man who could provide for you, and one who would enter into a lifelong covenant relationship.

Remember that sex is for marriage. If a guy is after sex, let him find it somewhere else. When you become the outlet for his hormonal urges—without a wedding ring—you cheapen yourself. You also lose all the power in the relationship. Practice self-control. Wait until the honeymoon.

CHAPTER FIVE

On Courtship and Dating

T rust in the Lord with all your heart and lean not on your own understanding; in all your ways acknowledge Him, and He will make your paths straight. (Proverbs 3:5-6)

God's plan for each person is different. Some will marry young. Some will wait. Some will never marry. The important thing is to seek God's will for your life first—to align yourself with God's word.

God doesn't want you to marry someone to "rescue" him. He wants you to marry a life partner with whom you can grow in your relationship with God.

Your Father in Heaven wants you to marry someone

who will provide a good home for you and your children. Because He loves you, God will provide a husband for you—in His time.

Before you date, ask God to direct your path, to help you make wise choices. Even just one date could be disastrous given the high incidence of date rape.

Trust in God. Trust that He will guide your steps. Lean on God's word. Read the Bible daily and learn about Him. Pray and ask for guidance. Acknowledge His supremacy in your life. Give your life to Him. He, who made you, who loves you more than you can ever know, will guide you. That is the promise He makes in Proverbs 3:5-6.

When is the right time to date or be courted? It's different for everyone. For some, sixteen years of age is right. Others will want to wait until they are eighteen or twenty. If you live under your parents' roof, ask them. If anyone knows you well enough to tell when you are ready, it's your parents.

If you are going to date, set boundaries—or ask your parents to set the boundaries for you. If you still live with your parents, invite your date in to meet them. Better yet, have the first date at your house with your parents. Or have him ask your father for permission to take you out to dinner. This acknowledges your father's authority and sets the tone for the relationship. Arrange for the man to spend some time alone with your father. Find out later what impression your father formed of this first visit.

The first few dates should be daytime events. It's okay to be alone with him, but be alone in a crowded restaurant, bowling alley, or skating rink. Dates to a golf course, the county fair, coffee-houses, shopping, book stores, and his parents' house for dinner are good choices. Dances, nightclubs, movies, and concerts are bad ideas until you get to know him and his intentions better. Go to places where the lights are on.

Don't drink alcohol. It will cloud your judgment and cause you to make choices you might not make if you were sober. Just one drink is too many. Don't drink while you are dating.

Tell him when you need to be home—regardless of whether or not there are parents waiting up for you. Make sure that he gets you home on time. If he doesn't, it indicates a lack of respect for your parents and a lack of respect for you. Don't say yes to a second date with him.

At the end of the evening, thank him for dinner. It sounds old-fashioned, but do not let him kiss you on the first date. Let him anticipate a kiss, maybe on a later date, maybe on your wedding day. Remember, you set the boundaries.

Do not call him the next day. If he gives you his number, tell him that you will wait to hear from him. Make him work to prove that he is interested in you—

that he is worthy of you. Don't call him unless you need to cancel a date.

When he calls you, be the one that ends the call. Don't let him hang up first. Tell him you have to go. End the call before he does. Don't worry, he'll call again. And again, and again—if you set the boundaries.

As the woman, you control the course that the relationship will follow. Set the boundaries and stick to them. A man will respect you for it.

My Father in Heaven, Be a light to my path. Help me to make wise choices. I trust you, Lord, because you love me more than I will ever know. Guide my steps. My life is Yours. I lean on Your word. I pray for wisdom and understanding. You are supreme in my life. I have given my life to You. Thank You for preparing a husband for me. Thank You for Your timing.

Amen.

CHAPTER SIX

The Test

You are beginning to see how important it is to apply logic to your relationships. Now use this test and the wisdom of the Book of Proverbs. Before you start the test, ask God to help.

The lamp of the Lord searches the spirit of a man;
it searches out his inmost being. (Proverbs 20:27)

You might look at the external characteristics mentioned in The Test, and think, "But God looks on the heart." That's true. But we don't have that ability. All we can do is look at external indications of inner conditions. Attitudes and actions come from within.

After you start the test, you may need to stop, go back and ask him questions about himself and his beliefs. That's okay, you're getting to know him better, and getting to know yourself. You're looking to the future and practicing wisdom.

Wisdom will save you from evil people, from those whose speech is corrupt. These people turn from right ways to walk down dark and evil paths. (Proverbs 2:12-13)

Read the whole question before answering. Possible answers are:

No	(N)
Yes	(Y)
Not Applicable	(N/A)
I Don't Know	(DK)

ATTITUDE

The most telling attribute of a fellow is his attitude. You can learn much just by looking at his posture and the way he interacts with others. Look a little closer and you'll learn more about him. Stop, look, and listen.

Answer

_____ 1. Is he quick to anger when he believes he has been slighted? *A fool shows his annoyance at once, but a prudent man overlooks an insult.* (Proverbs 12:16)

Do not make friends with a hot-tempered man, do not associate with one easily angered or you may learn his ways and get yourself ensnared. (Proverbs 22:24–25)

_____ 2. Does he laugh when someone gets hurt or is insulted? Is he delighted when the plans of others fail? *He who rejoices in calamity will not go unpunished.* (Proverbs 17:5 NASB)

_____ 3. Does he wear a habitual frown?

_____ 4. Is he boastful about the storehouse of knowledge that is his brain? A guy is quick to broadcast what he knows while a man doesn't make a show of his knowledge. *Pride goes before destruction, and a haughty spirit before stumbling.* (Proverbs 16:18 NASB)

_____ 5. Does he use foul language in daily conversation? If he talks that way around you, it's proof that he doesn't respect you. A man doesn't need to use profanity as a crutch.

_____ 6. Do you often hear him bragging? This is a good indication that he is not sure of himself. It comes down to attitude. Pick a man who is unsure of himself and he will never appreciate you for who you are. A man exhibits quiet self-confidence—though he might indulge in telling stories from time to time.

_____ 7. Does he display the middle finger of either hand to friends, enemies, or other drivers? Does he make other rude or obscene gestures or call people names? This kind of behavior is sure evidence of guy-hood. A man exhibits self-control and is mindful of others' feelings.

_____ 8. Is he afraid of the police or distrustful of authority? Does he refer to policemen as pigs, bacon, the fuzz, or any other derogatory term? A man respects authority and is not afraid of discipline. Fear of authority displays a guilty conscience.

AUTOMOBILE

A fellow's choice of car, truck, or motorcycle can tell you a lot. You can learn even more when you take a closer look at his vehicle—how he takes care of it, and how he drives it. Here's how:

_____ 9. Does he have cutout images of naked women reclining on his mud flaps? On the back of his car or truck does he have a picture of a rude little boy or a dog peeing on something? Does he have bumper stickers that communicate sexual undertones? Does he have a bumper sticker that proclaims the superiority of his vehicle over other manufacturers? Guys have obscene or rude bumper stickers. A man doesn't advertise contempt for others.

_____ 10. Does he shout at other drivers? Does he complain loudly when a slower driver pulls in front of him on the highway?

_____ 11. Does he drive a mud-caked truck around for a week after a Saturday playing off-road? Does he display the mud like a badge of his guy-hood?

_____ 12. Is his music so loud that the bass can be felt in the next car? Would he get mad if someone politely asked him to turn it down?

_____ 13. Has he ever honked the car horn to get you out of the house? A man will knock on the door and wait for you while you put the finishing touches on your lipstick. He will walk you to the car and hold the passenger door for you.

_____ 14. Do you get the feeling that he needs to have the newest/fastest car or the biggest/tallest truck? Does he park his motorcycle in the living room even though he has a garage? A man doesn't need to express his masculinity through his vehicle. He has relationships with people, not with objects.

FAMILY AND FRIENDS

Look at his family. What are they like? Does he have healthy, loving relationships with his parents, brothers, and sisters? Look at his friends. Friends are often a mirror of who he is. Watch carefully.

He who walks with wise men will be wise, but the companion of fools will suffer harm. (Proverbs 13:20 NASB)

_____ 15. Have you seen him ignore his father?
A wise son heeds his father's instruction, but a mocker does not listen to rebuke. (Proverbs 13:1)

Does he neglect his mother? *A foolish son brings grief to his father and bitterness to the one who bore him.* (Proverbs 17:25)

Does he dislike or show a lack of respect for your mother? Guys don't respect their mothers or your mother. Men love their moms and are—at the very least—polite to yours. If your guy is not, dump him now—even if your mom is hard to get along with. He will treat you the same way once you are married.

_____ 16. Does he hang out with the guys, drink beer, and tell dirty jokes? *A righteous man is cautious in friendship, but the way of the wicked leads them astray.* (Proverbs 12:26)

_____ 17. Does he date you while maintaining close relationships with other women? You know he's a guy if he won't give up his close relationships with female friends, even though he says he is serious about you.

_____ 18. Does he want you to keep working after your first child is born? If he can't support his family, he's not Mr. Right. A man knows his children need to be raised by parents, not babysitters, not pre-school teachers, not daycare providers. A man protects his wife and children and wants to be the provider for his family.

_____ 19. If he has children, does he neglect to discipline them? A man knows the consequences of not disciplining his children. *He who spares the rod hates his son, but he who loves him is careful to discipline him.* (Proverbs 13:24)

_____ 20. Does he tempt death? Does he crave extreme sports? You don't want to be worried about whether or not he'll come home alive. A man puts his family first.

_____ 21. If he is a father, does he spend more time with the guys than with his children? A guy would call spending time with his children, "baby-sitting." A man calls it family time. Real men invest time in their kids.

_____ 22. Does his former spouse/girlfriend have custody of the kids? Ask yourself why he was not awarded custody. Why didn't he fight to keep the marriage/relationship together for the sake of the children?

_____ 23. Does he delight in leading others astray, giving wrong advice for a joke? *The thoughts of the righteous are just, but the counsels of the wicked are deceitful.* (Proverbs 12:5 NASB)

FOOD AND DRINK

How he eats and drinks is often an indicator of his character. Does he eat or drink to excess? Does he eat unhealthy foods or healthy foods? It all makes a difference as you grow old together. *Like a city whose walls are broken down is a man who lacks self control.* (Proverbs 25:28)

_____ 24. Does he eat Fruit Loops for breakfast? Does he eat Cheetos for lunch? Does he eat Top Ramen for dinner? Does he neglect good nutrition? Chances are he neglects other key areas of his health as well.

_____ 25. Have you seen him overeat? Will he frequently eat more than he should? Does he take great pleasure in eating rich foods to excess? *Do not join those who drink too much wine or gorge themselves on meat, for drunkards and gluttons become poor, and drowsiness clothes them in rags.* (Proverbs 23:20-21)

_____ 26. Does he keep a lot of alcohol in the house? Have you seen him drunk? A man knows to stop drinking before losing control of his actions. *Who has woe? Who has sorrow? Who has strife? Who has complaints? Who has needless bruises? Who has bloodshot eyes? Those who linger over wine, who go to sample bowls of mixed wine.* (Proverbs 23:29–30)

GROOMING

How does he look? Would you be proud to introduce him to your parents, to your older brother, or your best friend? His grooming is a big indicator of his attitude.

_____ 27. Does he sport a pierced ear, navel, lip, tongue, eyebrow, nose, or nipple? A man doesn't need to express his individuality or group conformity in this way.

_____ 28. Has he paid to have a tattoo inscribed on his body within the last couple of years?

A man may have tattoos that he acquired in the military or while still a guy, but he doesn't continue to mark his body in this way.

_____ 29. Does he dye his hair and mustache? Does he wear a toupee? Does he wear colored contacts? If he is not comfortable with the color of his eyes, what else is he hiding? A man accepts the way God created him and is content.

_____ 30. Does he wear surplus army fatigues as casual wear?

_____ 31. Does he wear a T-shirt that says, "Wanted: One good woman that...," or any T-shirt with rude messages? Why is it that some guys have to advertise that they're low class? Thank him for the warning. Run the other way.

_____ 32. Does he wear excessive jewelry? An earring or earrings? A gaudy chain or bracelets? Does he wear pinky or toe rings, or even ankle bracelets? A man wears little jewelry: a watch, a wedding band and possibly a class ring, military, or other ring with significant meaning.

_____ 33. Does he wear his baseball cap backward more than forward? This can be a manifestation of rebellion.

_____ 34. Does he wear shorts or pants that hang down around his hips, allowing everyone to see his underwear? Have you seen him wear sloppy clothing in public when he had more appropriate clothes to wear? Does he slouch?

LIFESTYLE

What does he like to do in his spare time? There are a lot of clues here as to the quality of a future relationship you might have with him. Don't make the mistake of thinking you can change him after you get married. You can't.

_____ 35. Does he brag about practical jokes he's played on other people? Guys play practical jokes on other people and don't know when to quit.

_____ 36. Does he read *Playboy* or *Penthouse?* Does he say he likes the articles? Guys buy girlie magazines. Pay attention to what he reads. His bookshelf (if he has one) will give you a glimpse of who he is.

_____ 37. Have you seen him sit and watch professional wrestling? Not a good sign. Does he watch mindless sitcom drivel? Does he change channels constantly to see what he's missing on other channels? Men enjoy watching baseball, boxing, football, basketball, The History Channel, or fishing shows. Many men don't watch TV at all.

_____ 38. When he goes to a sporting event, does he shout at the referees? Even worse, does he shout at the refs on television?

_____ 39. Have you noticed pin-up posters of trucks, motorcycles, or scantily-clad women in his house? If a man has a poster, it's of a car, a motorcycle, or wildlife, and he'll pin it up in the garage.

_____ 40. Does he listen to music that affirms his guy-hood? The point: listen to the lyrics. If the lyrics support sex outside of marriage, drunkenness, drug use, or breaking the law, the music is feeding the wrong thing in your guy's heart. It's hard to get away from popular music in our culture, but if you see your fellow is stuck on one band or singer, listen to the message in the songs.

_____ 41. Does he make jokes at the expense of other people? Does he ridicule others for a laugh? *A man who lacks judgment derides his neighbor, but a man of understanding holds his tongue.* (Proverbs 11:12)

_____ 42. Do his favorite movies feed his mind on violence?

_____ 43. Is it important to him to have a drink with the boys after work? Would he choose to hang out with the guys more often than spending time with you or his family?

_____ 44. Does he abuse his body with excessive tobacco, alcohol, or illegal drugs? A man has control over his body and will not subject it to excessive use of damaging substances.

_____ 45. Did he quit learning when he got out of high school? A guy learns only enough to get by. A man continues to learn more about life and the world around him as he grows older. Of wisdom, Solomon wrote: *Long life is in her right hand; in her left hand are riches and honor. Her ways are pleasant ways, and all her paths are peace. She is a tree of life to those who embrace her; those who lay hold of her will be blessed.* (Proverbs 3:16-18)

But whoever fails to find me (wisdom) harms himself; all who hate me love death. (Proverbs 8:36)

____ 46. Is he unkind to animals? Does he neglect his pets? How he treats animals is a good indicator of who he is. If he neglects his pets, he'll neglect you. A man is concerned for the welfare of his animals. *A righteous man cares for the needs of his animal, but the kindest acts of the wicked are cruel.* (Proverbs 12:10)

____ 47. Have you heard it said of him that he sleeps in? *Do not love sleep or you will grow poor; stay awake and you will have food to spare.* (Proverbs 20:13)

MANNERS

How are his manners? Manners go back to attitude. Pay attention to how he behaves at dinner or in the company of others. Watch how he treats the people he meets and even the people he doesn't know.

_____ 48. Does he spit on the sidewalk as he walks down the street? Does he cough up phlegm in front of you? Yuck! This will only get worse! Next, he'll be blowing his nose without a tissue.

_____ 49. At dinner, does he use his pants to clean his hands? Or his shirt sleeve to wipe his mouth? Does he suck his teeth at the table after dinner? Does he use his fingernails to dig after meat stuck between his teeth?

_____ 50. Does he belch after eating? Do you have to remind him to say, "excuse me?" Belching is a signal that he lacks respect for you and those around him. Thank him for showing you his real self, then run.

_____ 51. Does he fail to really hear you when you

talk? Does he often ask questions about things that you've already told him? Get used to it. Many men are like that. But pay close attention anyway to this trait. If he loves you, he'll want to learn more about you. Men can be absent-minded. You have to learn the subtle difference between a lack of respect and absent-mindedness. If he doesn't listen to what you say, it's a sign of disrespect.

_____ 52. Does he forget people's names? Does he use the excuse that he cannot remember names? If he won't even try, it means he doesn't care about other people's feelings. He's a guy.

_____ 53. Does he leave the toilet seat up? Does he expect women to put the seat down when they have to use it? It's just a little thing—but it's an important little thing. If he respects you, he'll put it down.

_____ 54. Have you seen him litter? Does he throw an empty can out the window of his pickup? Not only is this illegal, it's inconsiderate. A man has respect for the land and the laws that govern our actions.

_____ 55. Does he forget to call when he's going to be late? Things can happen that will hold him up along the way. It's a fact of life. But a man will call if he can to let the other person know he's running behind. A guy won't make the effort.

_____ 56. Does he neglect to return phone calls? (Not your phone calls. You shouldn't be calling him, by the way) Watch carefully. A guy will just wait for the person to call again. A man will return the call—even if it is a salesman calling. He shows respect for the person who took the time to call.

_____ 57. Does he interrupt your conversations, or interject himself in the conversations of others uninvited? A guy thinks everyone is interested in what he has to say.

_____ 58. Does he forget to hold the door for you? He'd better not. Wait outside the car until he opens the door. Does he hold the door for other women? He'd better. Pay careful attention to how he treats women and even how he talks about women. If he doesn't respect women, put a lot of space between you and him and be quick about it.

MONEY AND TOYS

How he handles money is one of the best indicators of who he is. How he handles his finances will directly impact the quality of your life. Be very careful. Someone once said, "The difference between men and boys is the price of their toys." That is not entirely true. Some boys and guys have more money than is healthy for them. Men have toys too. The difference is in how they spend their money on the toys they buy. Does he buy the new jet-ski before paying the electric bill? Or does he buy a new car on credit when he is already having a hard time paying rent or paying off his school loans? That is an indicator of financial immaturity. *The rich rule over the poor, and the borrower is servant to the lender.* (Proverbs 22:7)

____ 59. Have you seen him buy on impulse? A man considers before making a purchase.

____ 60. Has he taken out a loan to buy a La-Z Boy Recliner or a big screen TV? Is he making payments on a jet-ski or motorcycle? A guy buys toys on credit. Does he accumulate debt? Remember this, a man accumulates assets, not liabilities.

____ 61. Does he buy you gifts on credit? Unless he pays off his credit card each month, he is borrowing money to buy your love. A guy like that will cause you pain. If he can't manage his money well enough to have cash on hand to buy you a gift, then he won't have enough money after you get married either. And don't let him borrow money to pay for your engagement ring either. A man saves his money over time to buy you a gift from his heart.

_____ 62. Does he always want to buy something bigger, faster, or better? Does he constantly compare what he has with others to see how he is doing? A guy is never satisfied with what he has. A man knows his manhood does not come from objects. It's okay for a man to buy things that he desires, but things should not be the focus of his manhood.

_____ 63. Is he always grasping for more money? Does he worry about having enough money for the future? Is he a workaholic? Never content? A man is thankful for what he has—he will work for the future, always hopeful for a better tomorrow, but he's content. *Do not wear yourself out to get rich; have the wisdom to show restraint.* (Proverbs 23:4)

_____ 64. Does his investment strategy consist of buying lottery tickets or pull-tabs, betting on football games, horse races, cockfights, or cards? They call that gambling. Hitching a ride through life with a gambler is a sure way to end up poor. *He who works his land will have abundant food, but he who chases fantasies lacks judgment.* (Proverbs 12:11)

_____ 65. Is he looking for instant gratification? Look at the things he spends his money on. Guys live in the present. A man saves his money for a future goal and spends his money sensibly. He should have a plan for the future. A man without a plan is not a man! *The plans of the diligent lead to profit as surely as haste leads to poverty.* (Proverbs 21:5)

_____ 66. Is he a co-signer on someone else's loan? Ask yourself why he is willing to take on another's debt? A man guards his finances and is not quick to open himself to unnecessary risk. *Do not be a man who strikes hands in pledge or puts up security for debts; if you lack the means to pay, your very bed will be snatched from under you.* (Proverbs 22:26-27)

RELATIONSHIPS

Watch how he treats others in his immediate family. Notice how they treat him. These are good clues as to how you'll be treated as a member of his family—both by him and by them.

He should consider your reputation and what others will think about you. *A good name is more desirable than great riches; to be esteemed is better than silver or gold.* (Proverbs 22:1) Does he value your moral convictions? Or does he make fun of them?

Is he devoted to you? Do his eyes sparkle when he talks to you? Can you tell he is in love?

Does he talk about the future? Can he handle commitment? If he is afraid of commitment, you should be afraid of him. Ask any single mother about guys who are afraid of commitment. Guys are not afraid of sex. Just consequences.

_____ 67. Has he ever raised his voice in an argument with you? Has he ever laid a hand on you in anger?

_____ 68. Does he bring flowers only when he wants to "make up?" A man will bring you flowers for the simple reason that he loves you and you deserve them.

_____ 69. Does he keep a "little black book." Does he watch other girls? In a social setting, does he pay undue attention to other women besides you? A real man is a "one-woman" man. If he ever had a black book, he threw it away when he met you.

_____ 70. Does he call you "the old lady?" If he does, chances are you have already cheapened yourself in his eyes.

_____ 71. Has he suggested you consider breast augmentation or a nose job? A man falls in love with who you really are, not who you pretend to be.

_____ 72. Have you seen that he never admits when he is wrong? Does he seek to lay blame on other people? A man can have a hard time admitting being wrong too, but he'll get around to it.

_____ 73. Does he whistle, leer, or honk at women? Is that how he met you? A man acknowledges an attractive woman with a smile, or looks away to keep his mind free from temptation.

_____ 74. Does he like you to dress in short skirts, low-cut blouses, and tight jeans so that other guys will whistle, leer, and honk at you?

_____ 75. Did he move quickly to try to get you into bed? A guy wastes no time bringing you to his room but a real man can wait until you say, "I do."

_____ 76. Does he hold grudges against other people? Is he bitter about wrongs done to him in the past? If he can't forgive, you'd better hope you never make a mistake. Change your phone number.

_____ 77. Does he make himself scarce when there is a job to be done?

_____ 78. Has he broken a promise to you? Has he broken a promise to someone else? A man keeps his word.

_____ 79. Does he believe you when you say, "you don't need to get me anything for my birthday?"

A man will buy you a "special something" anyway, knowing full well that you really don't mean it.

____ 80. Is he afraid to say the words, "I love you?" A man will tell you—but only if he means it.

____ 81. Does he care only for himself? Does he want much, yet give little of himself? *One man gives freely, yet gains even more; another withholds unduly, but comes to poverty. A generous man will prosper; he who refreshes others will himself be refreshed.* (Proverbs 11:24-25)

____ 82. Is his jealousy excessive? A man can be jealous of you or your time, but won't try to control you. The difference may be subtle, but there is a difference. Pay attention.

____ 83. Does he lie to you? Have you caught him in a fib, a white lie, an untruth, a half truth? Does he lie to his boss or his friends? *A lying tongue hates those it hurts, and a flattering mouth works ruin.* (Proverbs 26:28) Unraveling his lies is too much work. Let him lie to someone else.

RELIGION

Does he believe in God? Is his concept of God the same as yours? Does he attend the same church or do his beliefs contradict your own? The Bible tells us, *Do not be bound together with unbelievers; for what partnership have righteousness and lawlessness, or what fellowship has light with darkness?* (2 Corinthians 6:14 NASB). You may not think it's important now. But it will be when you have children. Pay close attention to his spiritual life. If it is different than yours, regardless of whether he is a man or just a guy, you're with the wrong one. Be equally yoked.

_____ 84. Is he attending church just because he wants to be with you? A guy goes to church because his girlfriend does. A man goes to church because he loves God and wants to learn more about Him.

_____ 85. Does he make fun of God-fearing, church-going friends or neighbors? Does he call them Bible-thumpers or religious freaks?

_____ 86. Does he try to change the subject when someone brings up the topic of religion or spirituality?

_____ 87. Does his Bible have a thick sheen of dust on top? A man goes to the word of God for guidance. *In the fear of the Lord there is strong confidence, and his children will have refuge.* (Proverbs 14:26 NASB)

_____ 88. Is God irrelevant to his life? A man who believes in God is afraid of displeasing Him. *Blessed is the man who always fears the Lord, but he who hardens his heart falls into trouble.* (Proverbs 28:14)

SPORTS

Someone said, "Sports do not build character, they reveal it." Most men and guys are passionate about sports. Watch how sports can reveal who he is.

_____ 89. Does he get into fights at baseball games? This kind of guy will embarrass you in front of your friends. When you have kids, he'll yell at your son when he strikes out and he'll pick a fight with the umpire.

_____ 90. Does he argue about the rules when his opponent is winning?

_____ 91. Does he cheat on his golf score?

_____ 92. When he plays ball sports, have you seen him be a ball hog? Does he want all the glory?

_____ 93. Does he get mad at others on his team that don't play as well as he does? A man recognizes that everyone has different limitations and skill levels.

_____ 94. Have you heard that he keeps more fish than his limit? Does he shoot game out of season? Does he hunt (poach) without a license? A man obeys game and fish laws and understands why the laws are in place.

_____ 95. When he gets home from a fishing trip, does he add 55% to the number and size of the fish he caught? (A man will only add 20%!) If he goes hunting, does he strap a deer head to his bumper and parade it around town? A man knows that this is offensive to most people.

_____ 96. Does he hunt big game or go fishing just for the trophy? Does he throw away the meat? Not only is that unethical, in most cases it's illegal. Men appreciate the hunt, the landscape, and the meat the animal provides.

WORK

He should work and contribute to society. He should not live off a trust fund or welfare. He should have a career path. Even if it changes from time to time. How he works—not what he does—can give you a good idea of the kind of person he is.

_____ 97. Does he skip from job to job, leaving when he gets bored or angry? Has he been fired more than once for being late, lazy, or not following directions? A man understands that he must work and earn his way in the world. *How long will you lie down, O sluggard? When will you arise from your sleep? A little sleep, a little slumber, a little folding of the hands to rest—And your poverty will come in like a vagabond, and your need like an armed man.* (Proverbs 6:9-11)

_____ 98. Does he have excuses for the things he hasn't done? A man has accomplishments and something to show for his work. *Lazy hands make a man poor, but diligent hands bring wealth.* (Proverbs 10:4)

____ 99. Does he often get angry when corrected? A guy can't take correction and doesn't like answering to authority figures. Men are accountable and appreciate constructive criticism. *Do not reprove a scoffer lest he hate you; Reprove a wise man and he will love you.* (Proverbs 9:8 NASB)

____ 100. Does he put off chores until it's too late? Is he disorganized and scattered? Look at how he spends his time. He should prioritize and take care of the important stuff first. If he is a procrastinator, it may not matter to you now, but it will matter later. *One who is slack in his work is brother to one who destroys.* (Proverbs 18:9)

In the end, it all comes down to attitude. You can tell a lot about a man by the way he looks at life and how he handles the difficulties life throws at him. You've been keeping score. You've learned some things about him. Total the points and turn to Chapter Seven. How does he score?

DIRECTIONS FOR SCORING

If the answer is *no*, score 0 points.

If the answer is *not applicable (N/A)*, score 0 points.

For *I don't know (DK)*, score 1 point.

For *yes,* score 2 points.

As in golf, the lower the score, the better.

How Does He Score?

0-10 Points A+

A big A+! An *A* for Applause, for Admiration. An *A* as in Accept his engagement ring (if you love him, of course).

You may have found an honorable man. Now go back and Analyze your answers. Did you cheat? Did you give unfair Advantage? Score him again before you proceed.

If he still scores just as high, date for at least a year before picking out the silverware. Read Chapter Eight. If you're still unsure about him, introduce him to your sister.

If you are already married to this wonderful man, tell him how much you Appreciate him. Tell him there is no one else like him. Fix his favorite meal and give him a big kiss when he gets home from work.

11-20 Points A

This is a good man. He may be your Mr. Right. Give it some time and go to God in prayer. Date for a year before accepting his ring and picking out names for the children. Read Chapter Eight on finding Mr. Right.

21-30 Points B+

He's a man but he has some guy qualities that should make you cautious. Share with him some of your concerns. Gauge his reaction, then proceed to Chapter Eight. If he is willing to work on his weaknesses, test him again after a year.

31-40 Points B

A big, bewildering *B*. *B* as in Be careful and Be cautious. Guys who score in this range sometimes make good friends. It's okay to go watch a baseball game with him, but don't go behind the Bleachers. Definitely, Be home Before 10:00 p.m. As nice as he MIGHT BE, he is, after all, still a guy.

He is growing up. BUT, he is not grown up. He may Become a man before too long. He has weaknesses, though. Keep an eye on him, but don't get too close. Score him again after a year.

41-60 Points C

A C-grade. *C* as in average. *C* as in Calamity. *C* as in Childish Clod, Conceited, Crude, Crooked, Convict, Combative, Contentious. *C* as in Consequences, Complications, and CONTRACEPTION (the best contraceptive is saying NO!). A *C* as in Curtains. Show him the door! Give this guy about five years. He may turn into a man, though I wouldn't hold my breath. Forget him and find someone else. Guys like this won't change just because you marry them. They'll only grow up when enough quality women—LIKE YOU—tell them where to get off. Don't try to rescue him from guy-hood. You'll only be sorry.

61-80 Points D

A big *D*. *D* as in Divorce waiting to happen. *D* as in Downright Dangerous Dude. If you're already married to him, start praying—hard. Then turn to the Appendix and read "What To Do If You're Already Married To A Guy." Don't have children until he can score at least a *B* on this test.

If you're not married yet, hit the road. If you're engaged, give him the ring back. Don't waste your time. He'll only ruin your life.

81-200 Points F

An *F*! *F* as in Flunked. *F* as in Failure. *F* as in Faithless, and *F* as in leave no Forwarding address. *F* as in Fatal to your happiness. He Flunked and you wasted your time taking this test, because you knew he was a guy before you started. There is no chance that he will get a passing grade anytime soon. You already knew that he was no good.

If you're married to him, turn to the Appendix and read "What To Do If You're Already Married To A Guy." Start working on your education and marketable skills. Don't have any children! If you already have children with him, start training them how to make better decisions than you did.

If you're shacking up, move out while he's at work (if he has a job). Leave a note, but no Forwarding Address.

If you're engaged, break it off. Chances are he didn't let you set a date anyway.

If he is picking you up for a date on Friday, schedule a tooth extraction or an IRS audit instead.

CHAPTER EIGHT

Is He Mr. Right?

Y ou've tested him. You have scored him. If he made the grade, you may be contemplating the next step. Is he a good man? Here's a good summary of how to tell:

A good man is honest. If you find him in a lie or an act of deception of any form, walk away and don't look back. You may turn into a pillar of salt if you do and live in misery for the rest of your life.

A good man is loving. A mate should love you as much as he loves himself. If you find that the pendulum swings mainly towards him, get away fast. A happy, healthy marriage cannot exist when self-love or self-pity outweighs his ability to love another.

A good man is respectful. If he is quick to ask you to share his bed, he's not worth it. Not only will sleeping with him before you are married ruin your relationship, it will lessen his respect for you.

A good man has quality friendships. If he can have a good time with his friends without getting drunk or watching scantily clad girls, there's hope. Most often you can find out the quality of a guy or man by looking at the kind of people he hangs out with.

A good man respects himself. Does he take care of himself? Does he dress with care? Does he pay his way? Does he have plans for his future? And does he love the Lord? If not—run fast. You will be taking care of him and paying his way for the rest of your life.

The book of (Proverbs says that whoever walks with the wise will become wise, and whoever walks with fools will suffer harm. Trouble will follow you the rest of your days if you choose to settle for just another guy. Blessings will follow if you choose your man with care and prayerful consideration.

A man is not a man because of his age or his physical characteristics. A man is a man when he has honor, when he has honorable plans, when he treats other people with respect, when he pays his own way, and when he has self-control.

Is he the right man? Don't trust your feelings. Feelings can lie. And love can make us stupid. Trust logic instead.

What does your head tell you? What do your friends tell you? What do your mother and father tell you? Have you ever heard the expression, love is blind? Recognize that you may have blinders on. Ask a trusted friend what she thinks.

Examine his interests. Do you share them? Could

you learn to be interested in what he enjoys? Will you support him in the pursuit of his dreams?

Ask yourself if the culture that he comes from is compatible with yours. Are your dreams and plans for the future agreeable? Do you share the same religious values? Is his relationship with God growing?

If you are willing to help each other, to serve each other as you embark on this great adventure together, your home will be filled with the peace, prosperity, and abundance that God has in store for you.

There is One who knows us better than we know ourselves. He is God. He loves you more than you can imagine, and He desires a relationship with you.

Put God first in your life and He will be a lamp to your feet and a light to your path. He will be the Architect of your future, if you let Him.

Let love and faithfulness never leave you; bind them around your neck, write them on the tablet of your heart. Then you will win favor and a good name in the sight of God and man. (Proverbs 3:3-4)

You are a gift from God to him. *A prudent wife is from the Lord.* (Proverbs 19:14b)

God says that you are worth much to the man you marry. By giving the right man the honor of having you for a wife, you offer him happiness, wealth, and honor.

He who finds a wife finds what is good and receives favor from the Lord. (Proverbs 18:22)

A wife of noble character who can find? She is worth far more than rubies. (Proverbs 31:10)

Her husband is respected at the city gate, where he takes his seat among the elders of the land. (Proverbs 31:23)

Be that woman of noble character.

On Marriage

Wedding, *n.* 1. The act or ceremony of marrying, with its attendant festivities. 2. The anniversary of a marriage or its celebration. 3. Harmonious blending or association. *The Random House Dictionary.*

I think number three is the best definition. A harmonious blending. That is what marriage should be—though we can all think of hundreds of examples of blends (marriages) that turned out to be less than harmonious.

The reason that many marriages don't work is

because—in every case—one or both partners do not work at the marriage.

Marriage takes work. It takes commitment to the concept of marriage and commitment to each other. When you marry a man who is committed to you for life—when you commit to him for life, for richer or for poorer, for better or worse, in sickness and health, till death do you part—you can smile at the future, knowing your marriage will be a harmonious blending.

Expect your marriage to be as good in ten, twenty, thirty, forty, fifty, or even sixty years as it was on the day you made your vows.

Commit to dating your spouse regularly after the ceremony. Don't let the busyness of life interfere with your relationship.

Stay connected physically. Go for walks in the evening. Ride bicycles together or play tennis. Build your memories together. Staying connected physically is important to your emotional connection.

Kiss. Hug. Touch. Hold hands. Don't let him leave the house without a kiss. Don't let him come home without kissing you as soon as he walks in the door. Before you close your eyes to sleep, kiss again. If he forgets remind him. He'll love you for it.

Sex is vital to the health of your marriage. It was given to you by God as a gift to help you connect to your partner. Make love often.

Practice serving him. Make his lunch before work. And put a little note in to remind him of you in the middle of the day. Serving him will make him want to dote on you. It really works.

Be the woman that God wants you to be. Be the woman that your man needs. Build him up when he's down. *The wise woman builds her house, but with her own hands the foolish one tears hers down.* (Proverbs 14:1)

Keep communications open. When he needs to talk, be there for him. When you need him, he'll be there for you. Never stop talking to each other. It's vital to your relationship.

When you disagree or argue, don't let the little things become big things. Don't let the sun go down on your wrath. Talk it out and don't go to sleep without making up—and have fun making up!

Sit down at dinner together. Laugh together. Cry together. But whatever you do—do it together.

Commit to the Lord whatever you do, and your plans will succeed. (Proverbs 16:3)

What To Do If You're Already Married To A Guy

Perhaps you are already married. It's common for girls to marry first, then apply logic to the relationship after the excitement of picking out a wedding dress, saying "I do" and opening the gifts.

What do you do when you finally realize that you married a guy?

Take heart. A lot of guys will grow up and turn into men. But in the ideal scenario, he grows up before you marry him.

You got married too soon. Don't compound one error by making more mistakes. Don't have children until your guy becomes a man. Having a child will not make him a man.

Don't ever give up on your marriage. Be the best partner you can be.

If you have children already or have one on the way, commit to being the best parent you can be. Raise your children to understand the concept of delayed gratification. Teach them that everything should come in its proper time.

As for you, educate yourself—through correspondence courses, classes at the community college, and books. Teach yourself marketable skills. Marriage to a guy is uncertain.

Never give up. Remember the vows you made before God.

Be the best wife you can be. Pray for your husband every day and tell him how much you love him. Be the attractive, vivacious girl he married, but grow up and start making better decisions. Marriage is for life. You married a guy, but he may yet grow into a man.

Suggested Reading List

The Book of Proverbs

Ecclesiastes

Song of Solomon

1 Corinthians 13

Ten Stupid Things Women Do To Mess Up Their Lives
   by Dr. Laura Schlessinger